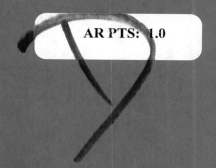

WILDFIRES

WILDFIRES

BY ANN ARMBRUSTER

A FIRST BOOK

Franklin Watts
A Division of Grolier Publishing
New York   London   Hong Kong   Sydney
Danbury, Connecticut

Cover and Interior Design Adaptation by Molly Heron

Photographs ©: James C. Smalley: cover, chapter openers, pp. 11, 15, 16, 17, 21, 26, 28, 29, 36, 38, 51, 57; Bettmann Archive: pp. 6, 39; Comstock: pp. 2, 22, 44; Courtesy of Forest History Society, Durham, NC: p. 19; Gamma-Liaison: pp. 13 (Brad Markel), 55 (Benali-Gifford); Marine Independent Journal: p. 53; UPI/Bettmann: pp. 24, 27, 33, 34, 40; USDA Forest Service: pp. 31, 32, 46; Yellowstone National Park: pp. 9, 43, 48.

Library of Congress Cataloging-in-Publication Data

Armbruster, Ann.
    Wildfires / by Ann Armbruster.
        p. cm. — (A First book)
    Includes bibliographical references (p.) and index.
    Summary: Explains wildfires and their causes, explores the dangers and benefits of wildfires, and provides information on fire-fighting methods and the special problems encountered when wildfires strike populated areas.
    ISBN 0-531-20250-X
    1. Wildfires—Juvenile literature. 2. Forest fires—Juvenile literature. 3. Fire ecology—Juvenile literature. [1. Wildfires. 2. Forest fires. 3. Fire ecology. 4. Ecology.] I. Title. II. Series.
    SD421.23.A75 1996   96-13551 CIP AC
    363.37'9—dc20

CONTENTS

1

A FORCE OF NATURE

From the earliest times, wildfires have been a source of wonder and fear. Imagine the terror of primitive people when a forest burst into flames. Even today, photographs and television images of wildfires fill our twentieth-century minds with awe.

Humankind is both fascinated and repelled by fire. It cooks our food, heats our homes, makes glass, metals, and pottery. Fire is used in our scientific projects and in our religious rituals. It is essential to civilization, and it is part of our everyday lives.

Fire also destroys property and threatens our safety. The fire that cooks the hamburgers on the grill can burn our home. That crackling glow in the fireplace can reduce our belongings to blackened debris. This unpredictable force of nature causes misery as well as joy.

Many myths and legends exist about the discovery of fire. In ancient Greece they told the story of Prometheus, a Greek

Prometheus gives fire to humans.

Titan who stole fire from the gods and gave it to humans. As punishment, Prometheus was chained to a rock. Each day, an eagle was sent to peck out his liver, which grew back to its full size each night. He was finally freed from his punishment by the Greek hero, Hercules.

Many ancient myths depict animals as the givers of fire. These animals often overcome tremendous difficulties to bring fire to human beings. Long ago, the North American Paiute Indians told such a legend. In their story, a young Indian boy and his friend, Coyote, the wily hero featured in numerous American Indian tales, saw people suffering from the winter cold. Coyote wanted to help them, so he told the boy how to bring fire back from the Burning Mountain located in the West. This dramatic tale relates how brave Coyote, the boy, and one hundred fast runners carried fire from the Burning Mountain to the Paiute people. After this brave deed, Coyote was called the Fire Bringer.

As our knowledge of fire has increased, we have learned that burning and clearing the land brings fresh plant growth, makes travel easier, and makes hunting more effective. Anthropogenic fires—fires set by humans—have changed some forests into prairies.

American Indians have known about the benefits and dangers of fire for centuries. In American Indian tradition, fire is sometimes called Grandfather Fire as a sign of awe and respect. Smoke signals were used for communication in wartime, and American Indians often set fire to the prairies to force their enemies out of hiding, making them easier to attack. They protected themselves from wildfires by burning large areas of brush and building their houses in the

Animals seeking fresh plant growth in recently burned spaces were easy targets for American Indian hunters and trappers.

middle of the burned space that was now free of flammable material.

American Indians used fire most commonly for hunting. The smoke from fire brought bears out of their caves and raccoons out of their dens. American Indians would also set fire to grasslands to attract animals to the fresh grass that shoots up after a fire. In the newly cleared spaces, the animals were easy targets for hunters and trappers. In the early nineteenth century, explorers Lewis and Clark observed this practice in the upper Missouri River valley. They wrote, "Every spring the plains are set on fire and the buffalo are tempted to cross the river in search of the fresh grass which immediately succeeds the burning." The buffalo would then be isolated on ice floes in the river, making them defenseless against the approaching hunters.

When the Pilgrims arrived in North America in 1620, they engaged in massive burnings of the forests to clear the land for farming. The clearings also served as protection against American Indian attacks. American settlers derived many benefits from forested lands. They built wooden homes, wooden fences, and used wood as their primary fuel. Wood was essential to their lifestyle, and trees were cut down with little regard for conservation. They treated the country's forests as though they would last forever.

As the twentieth century drew near, however, a lumber crisis in Europe sparked national concern about our dwindling forests. U.S. president Theodore Roosevelt set aside large portions of forestland that later became national parks, and in 1905, Congress created the United States Forest Service, headed by Gifford Pinchot. Under his guidance, the concept of forestry was introduced. Forestry is the science of maintaining and developing forests. Foresters protect the trees, soil, and wildlife of the forest and prescribe methods of lumbering that preserve the forests' long-term health. They fight against insects, disease, irresponsible logging, and fire.

Wildfires can be a tremendous threat to our forests, causing catastrophic damage in a short period of time. In the United States, more than three hundred forest fires occur each day. Today, foresters watch for fires from lookout towers

A wildland firefighter watches a blaze from the safety of a fire line.

and fight them with modern equipment. They also educate people about the importance of protecting our forests. But does protecting our forests mean extinguishing wildfires in all cases? In addition to understanding the destructive nature of forest fires, modern foresters try to understand how periodic fires can be part of a healthy, natural cycle of forest regeneration.

A WILDFIRE IS BORN

Most of us have vivid memories of fire—a roaring fire in a fireplace, a bonfire celebration before a sports event, or a glowing campfire. Thinking back, we remember the smell of smoke, the intense heat, and red and orange flames dancing in all directions.

Now imagine a lightning bolt sizzling down a tree trunk or a careless camper abandoning a still-smoldering campfire. Wisps of smoke appear, leaves ignite, and flames spread to nearby brush and trees. A wildfire is born.

TYPES OF FIRES

Wildfire spreads wherever it comes in contact with suitable fuel. Some fires burn out of control for days while others fizzle

A surface fire

out in a short time. The duration of the fire depends on the weather and availability of fuel.

A fire that burns beneath the surface of the forest floor is called a ground fire. These slow-burning fires are fueled by the decaying organic material—peat moss and leaves, for example—that lies just underground. They produce a lot of smoke, but because of the limited oxygen in the dense underground fuels, they do not produce much heat in comparison to other fires. Ground fires move erratically through the forest floor, sometimes burning for hours, days, or weeks. Ground fires that come in contact with coal seams can travel miles underground, sometimes undetected for months.

A ground fire can quickly become a surface fire if it ignites surface materials. Surface fires are the most common type of wildfire. They burn the vegetation and debris on the forest floor but usually do little damage to trees. Since surface fuels are less compacted and are surrounded by more oxygen than the subsurface fuels that feed ground fires, surface fires give off more heat and burn more quickly than ground fires. Nevertheless, surface fires can smolder for hours before flames appear.

The most destructive type of wildfire is the crown fire, which attacks the crowns, or tops, of trees. If a fire ladder is present (dry branches or small trees leading to the tops of taller trees), a surface fire can quickly develop into a crown fire. These fires travel rapidly from treetop to treetop.

By climbing the dry branches of a tree, such as this pine, a surface fire can become a crown fire.

Trees explode into flames. The fire can now travel from treetop to tree-top, especially if fanned by high winds.

A forest fire rages in the background, leaving charred trees in its path.

Crown fires do not stay in one place very long. When fanned by high winds, the flames literally jump from one tree-top to another, often destroying everything in their path. Strong winds can carry the fire across water or cleared land to other areas. Taming these fires is one of the biggest challenges forest firefighters must face. In fact, some crown fires are uncontrollable under extreme conditions.

Large and violent crown fires are called firestorms or "blowups." These massive fires often contain destructive indrafts and strong, swirling winds similar to those of a tornado. As a firestorm spreads, treetops are snapped off, hats are pulled off firefighters' heads, and everything loose is sucked into the advancing inferno. Day is turned into night as thick, black smoke obscures almost all sunlight.

Firestorms are dangerous and unpredictable. During a 1967 firestorm in the Selkirk Mountains of northern Idaho, flames advancing at 80 miles per hour (130 km/hr) toppled trees 60 to 75 feet (18 to 23 m) high. The peak fire intensity of the storm was estimated to be equal to the explosion of a 2,000-kiloton nuclear bomb.

NOTABLE FIRES

Great Peshtigo Fire of 1871   The deadliest forest fire disaster in the United States occurred on October 8, 1871, in Peshtigo, Wisconsin. It claimed the lives of 1,200 people. The fire ravaged 2,400 acres (970 hectares) of Wisconsin woodlands. Many panic-stricken Peshtigo residents saved themselves by jumping into the Peshtigo River, which ran through the middle of town. One observer wrote: "In less than five minutes there was fire everywhere. The atmosphere quickly got unbearably warm, and the town was enveloped by a rush of air as hot as though it were issued from a blast furnace. The wind lifted the roofs on houses, toppled chimneys, and showered the town with hot sands and live coals."

The Great Black Dragon Fire   On May 6, 1987, forest fires burned throughout vast areas of northern China and the

The Great Peshtigo Fire ravages a Wisconsin home.

former Soviet Union for nearly a month. The fires destroyed 3.2 million acres (1.3 million hectares) in China and another 15 million acres (6.1 million hectares) in Siberia. Though few people in the Western world have heard of this natural disaster, it was the largest forest fire in recorded history.

No foreign correspondents were permitted to observe the Great Black Dragon Fire. No reports were allowed on the fire until the fall of 1987 when the Chinese government permitted Harrison Salisbury, a former *New York Times* reporter, to enter the region and write a book about the fire.

The Yellowstone Fires, 1988   In the summer of 1988, eight huge fires raged through 1.4 million acres (567,000 hectares) of Yellowstone National Park's 2.2 million acres (890,000 hectares). Some of the fires were caused by lightning, some by human carelessness. Extreme drought conditions and high winds helped the fires advance, some as much as 14 miles (23 km) per day. On August 20 alone, the Yellowstone fires covered 165,000 acres (67,000 hectares), more forestland than had burned since the park's creation in 1872. This day was appropriately nicknamed Black Saturday.

At one time, 9,500 firefighters, working with helicopters, bulldozers, and hand tools, battled the wind-driven flames. The total cost of the Yellowstone fires was $120 million, the highest in U.S. fire-fighting history. Helicopters, costing $1,700 per hour, flew 18,000 hours, dropped 10 million gallons (38 million liters) of water, and 1.4 million gallons (5.3 million liters) of fire retardant. Twenty-five thousand firefighters and four thousand troops worked to extinguish the blazes. One bystander observed, "[Looking] at the firestorms, you would have thought nothing would survive."

Yellowstone National Park, 1988

CAUSES OF FOREST FIRES

Before a fire can break out, three elements must come together in the same area: fuel, oxygen, and a heat source. The combination of these three components is called a fire triangle, and a fire cannot exist in the absence of any one of them.

Fuel for wildfires generally consists of dry vegetation, which includes bushes, underbrush in a forest, or trees. Drought (a period of dry weather resulting from far below normal rainfall) can contribute to the buildup of dry material. Forest and grass fires spread quickly when there are higher than normal temperatures and very dry conditions.

The oxygen necessary to sustain a wildfire is already present in the atmosphere. Loosely packed fuels above ground allow more oxygen to mingle with the fuel. Consequently, fires fed by these fuels burn hotter and faster than fires that are fed by denser, subsurface fuels.

The final part of the fire triangle, a heat source, is supplied by a natural event or by humans. Mother Nature can provide a heat source in many ways. The hot ash and lava from an erupting volcano can start a fire. In addition, earthquakes and high winds can knock down electric power lines, setting a forest ablaze. The most common natural heat source, however, is lightning from ordinary thunderstorms. Close to 75 percent of a lightning bolt's energy is changed to heat during a lightning discharge. Scientists rate lightning bolts as either hot or cold strokes. A cold stroke of lightning is of short duration. A hot stroke of lightning (referred to as LLC, for long-lasting current) is more likely to start a fire.

While nature is responsible for starting some fires, people provide the heat source for about nine out of ten forest fires in the United States. A driver carelessly discards a cigarette and the sparks ignite the surrounding dry vegetation. Or, a fire can start from the smoldering ashes produced when a homeowner burns a pile of leaves. Sometimes, wildfires are even set deliberately by arsonists.

Lightning is the most common natural cause of wildfires.

FIGHTING WILDFIRES

Firefighters are taught to remove the three components of the fire triangle quickly in order to suppress a fire. They try to remove the fuel sustaining a fire, diminish the source of oxygen that is feeding a fire, and lower the temperature of the heat source.

Firefighters remove the fuel contributing to a forest fire by cutting a fire line or control line. As the fire approaches, workers cut down trees and remove any easily ignited material in a line crossing the anticipated path of the fire. This action creates a fuel gap that the fire cannot cross. In some instances, crews will try to create a fire line where there are natural barriers, such as a lake or a clearing in the forest.

Fire crews often resort to backfires as a firefighting method. A backfire is a small fire that is set directly in the path of a large fire. It burns toward the advancing wildfire and consumes the brush and vegetation in the larger fire's path,

A fire-fighting crew in Yellowstone National Park cuts a fire line through dense underbrush with tools called Pulaskis.

A firefighter sets a backfire with a drip torch.

depriving the wildfire of its fuel. With backfires, firefighters literally fight fire with fire.

When battling a wildfire, firefighters also try to deprive the fire of its oxygen source. The most common means of doing this is by pouring water on the fire. As water is converted to steam by the heat of the fire, the steam creates a barrier between the flames and the oxygen-rich air in the atmosphere. Water is also used to cool the heat source contributing to a fire. The water, as it changes to steam, absorbs heat from its surroundings, thereby lowering the temperature of the heat source. This slows the progress of the fire.

In recent years, fire researchers have developed various fire retardants. One of these, called "wet water," is made of

A firefighter extinguishes a flare-up.

Foam clings to potential fuel, such as these dry leaves, better than plain water.

water mixed with special fire-retardant foams. This thick mix-ture clings to fuels better than conventional water and covers the fuel with a fire-resistant film. Fire-retardant foams cool fires and reduce the fire's oxygen supply for longer periods of time than plain water. Today, planes and helicopters drop thousands of gallons of water mixed with fire-retardant chemi-cals on fires, creating nonflammable fuel barriers in front of

A plane drops fire retardant on a wildfire.

an advancing fire. Foam is also frequently distributed through foam-generator pumps. Some fire retardants are colored bright red. This enables pilots to see what portion of a fire area they have covered.

WILDFIRE FIGHTERS

There are two major crews of firefighters dedicated to fighting wildfires. They are called Smokejumpers and Hotshots.

Smokejumpers Smokejumpers are elite crews, employed by the U.S. Forest Service and the Bureau of Land Management, that parachute into remote mountain wildernesses to fight wildfires. These highly trained firefighters have been jumping out of planes to fight fires since 1940.

Smokejumper training is rigorous, making great physical and mental demands. In the first week 50 percent of the applicants drop out. Smokejumpers learn how to jump out of a plane, how to make safe landings, and how to free themselves from parachutes. They wear heavily padded jumpsuits made of lightweight, fire-resistant material to protect themselves from smoke and flames. Smokejumpers must be in superb physical condition since they carry equipment that weighs 85 pounds (39 kg) and must often cover hazardous territory.

Hotshots The Hotshots are another elite fire-fighting crew employed by the Forest Service. These ground crews wear hard hats and gloves. They carry canteens, a backpack, a bandana to breathe through, and safety glasses to protect their eyes.

Hotshots work in twenty-person crews, and each crew, with its colorful hats, is proud of its reputation. As one Hotshot member proudly states, "Remember, a Hotshot crew goes where no other will go and works longer than any other crew will work."

In addition to Hotshots and Smokejumpers, there are ground crews that play an important part in mopping up controlled fires. The mop-up phase of fire fighting is perhaps the dirtiest and most tiresome job. Ground crews enter the burned areas to look for hot spots—charred logs or any other potential heat sources that might reignite a forest fire. If any are found, the crew douses them with water or dirt.

Smokejumpers descending over an Alaska fire

A Hotshot crew member

No matter which crew a firefighter works on, battling wild-fires takes a tremendous toll on the body. Inhaling smoke while working on a fire line for a day is equivalent to smoking four packages of cigarettes.

FIRE-FIGHTING TOOLS

Today, new techniques and tools are available to help firefighters detect a wildfire and arrive quickly at the scene. The traditional forest ranger in a lookout tower now receives assistance from people in helicopters.

A firefighter runs from a flaming tree trunk he just cut down during the mop-up phase of a Yellowstone National Park fire.

Helicopters are used to help spot a fire, determine the location, radio information back to headquarters, and transport fire crews to the fire site in minutes. These helicopters can drop hundreds of gallons of water on a fire and refill their tanks immediately. They are also used for laying hose. As the helicopter flies forward, the hose is gradually released. Previously, it took eight firefighters thirty minutes to lay 1,500 feet (457 meters) of hose up a medium slope. It takes a helicopter only about fifty seconds.

Fire detection is also easier than it was in years past because of the development of the infrared camera. Infrared rays are a type of invisible radiation that is emitted to some degree by all objects. The intensity of the rays varies according to the temperature of the object they come from. Though the rays cannot be seen by the human eye, infrared cameras can detect this radiation and map temperature differences in a particular area. By assigning colors to each temperature, the cameras can provide images even in complete darkness, or when conditions make conventional cameras useless. For example, when mounted on helicopters and flown over a fire site, infrared cameras can pinpoint the location of the fires by detecting the areas of higher temperature—even when layers of smoke obscure the fires completely from human eyes. After aerial images are taken of the trouble spots and transferred

This helicopter can drop water on a fire and refill its tank in minutes.

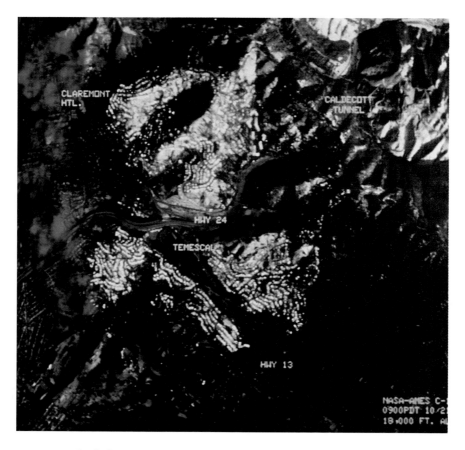

Labels in image: CLAREMONT HTL., CALDECOTT TUNNEL, HWY 24, TEMESCAL, HWY 13, NASA-AMES C-, 0900PDT 10/2, 18,000 FT. A

An infrared image of a fire area in Oakland, California

to the nearest command post, the Forest Service uses the infrared images to map fires and locate hot spots.

Compared to their predecessors, today's Smokejumpers and Hotshot crews have more powerful water pumps, better first-aid equipment, larger supplies of food, and more sophisticated two-way radios at their disposal. The most common tool, however, has been around since the turn of the century. Called a Pulaski, it is a tool that combines an ax with a hoe, and it is excellent for slashing underbrush and chopping bushes. It is named for Edward Pulaski, a ranger who made the first model in 1903.

Sometimes firefighters are cut off from the rest of the crew, trapped by blazing trees and brush. The Forest Service has developed a portable fire shelter to protect firefighters in these life-threatening situations. Made of aluminum foil bonded to a thin fiberglass cloth, the shelter is the size of a folded-up newspaper and unfolds into a small tent in less than twenty seconds. As a fire approaches, the firefighters lie flat on the ground underneath the shelter, and for brief periods of time, the shelter can protect its users from temperatures as high as 1,600°F (871°C). These shelters, sometimes called shells because they are so light and thin, are especially effective against explosive fires that sweep across a wooded area very quickly, giving the firefighters no time to escape. Such fires frequently leave an area as quickly as they arrive, but they are especially deadly without the aid of the fire shelters. Firefighters have nicknamed this life-saving device "shake and bake," and hope they never have to use one.

On August 29, 1985, a forest fire in Salmon National Forest in Idaho trapped seventy-three firefighters. All were saved by their fire shelters. Unfortunately, the fire shelters do not eliminate all the dangers firefighters face in the forest.

In the summer of 1994, a wildfire near Glenwood Springs, Colorado, killed fourteen firefighters. The fire spread from 50 acres (20 hectares) to 2,000 acres (809 hectares) in less than three hours. Though it started as a small, contained fire, it exploded when it encountered wind gusts in excess of 50 miles

A firefighter unfolds a fire shelter.

per hour (80 km/hr). "It felt like a blowtorch," said one Smokejumper who survived. Nine of the survivors were saved by their fire shelters. Some of the victims, however, were also in their shells. Intense fires can overwhelm even the fire shelters.

Interior Secretary Bruce Babbitt expressed the country's sorrow: "This is a great tragedy involving the finest fire-fighting

A memorial honoring the fourteen firefighters killed near Glenwood Springs, Colorado

crews this country has ever produced. These guys can handle just about everything. But going after a fire is not risk free."

SMOKEY BEAR

Keeping in mind that 90 percent of wildfires in the United States are started by humans, the most effective means of fighting fires is to be more aware of our roles in starting and preventing fires. Responsibility is a more effective means of controlling forest fires than the most sophisticated fire-fighting equipment.

This issue first received national attention in 1945 when one of the most famous cartoon characters in United States history became a symbol for forest-fire prevention. Smokey Bear appeared bearing the message, "Only YOU Can Prevent Forest Fires."

In 1950, a real bear cub was found clinging to a tree after a fire ravaged a New Mexico forest. The orphaned bear was named Smokey, and he became the living symbol of forest fire prevention. He spent his days at the National Zoo in Washington, D.C., until his death in 1976. Smokey has heightened public awareness of fire dangers, and forest fire damage has decreased by 80 percent since his appearance.

The real Smokey Bear is made an honorary member of the Washington, D.C., Fire Department. Smokey is feeling a bit rambunctious, so the deputy fire chief keeps his distance.

FIRE ECOLOGY

Until the 1970s, the National Park Service and the United States Forest Service followed a policy of fighting most natural fires. As they learned more about wildfires, experts recognized that in many cases fire must be allowed to burn in wild places to restore the balance of nature. They understood that by extinguishing *all* forest fires, we disrupt important natural cycles in our forests.

Ecology is a science that is a branch of biology. It is the study of relationships between living things and their environment. Fire ecology is the study of how people, animals, and plants live with fire, which is part of our natural environment. Though wildfires have traditionally been regarded as entirely destructive, fire ecologists today suggest that the role of these controversial fires is much more complex.

Ecologists acknowledge that wildfires have been a natural force on the planet for millions of years. They accept fire as part of the environment just as they accept sunshine and rain All of these forces can be destructive at times, but all are vital to our survival. Although fire can be devastating, much of the Earth's plant and animal life thrives under the influence of periodic fires.

Fresh growth after a fire provides food for plant-eating animals.

When a fire sweeps through a forest, it burns off the duff, or decaying material such as fallen logs, tree limbs, and leaves that accumulate on the forest floor. The nutrients from the burned material enrich the soil and encourage new growth. Fire can also thin the thick canopy of leaves that usually prevents sunlight from reaching new growth on the forest floor. Soon grass, shrubs, and flowers appear in the burned-out area. For plant-eating animals, such as elk and deer, the end of a forest fire means a plentiful and more nutritious food supply. After a fire, the new plant growth is richer in nutrients such as phosphate, calcium, and protein. Wildlife returns to feed on the new source of food.

This lodgepole pine forest depends on periodic fires for its survival. The pink flowers are also a fire species. They are named fireweed because they spread so quickly over freshly burned areas.

FIRE SPECIES

Many living things survive and benefit from wildfires. It is now known that some plants and animals even depend on fire for survival. These plants and animals are called fire species, and many have adapted methods of encouraging fires in their environment.

Many of the pine trees that grow in the highlands of the western United States are fire species. These trees, which include the ponderosa pine and the lodgepole pine, have seeds that are surrounded by a highly flammable resin that must be melted before the seeds can pop out. The needles of these trees decay slowly on the forest floor and seem born to burn. They provide ample fuel for periodic fires, without which the pine forests would die.

In southern California, the chaparral, a dense growth of shrubs and small trees, also drops seeds that must be cracked open by intense heat. Fortunately for the chaparral, the hot, dry summers and high winds in California create ideal conditions for wildfires, and the chaparral itself is excellent fuel.

The firehawk, an Australian predator, starts its own fires. This bird actually flies into a fire, grabs a burning twig, and drops it into unburned grass. When the grass ignites, rodents and other prey are flushed out of their hiding places and provide easy hunting for the firehawk.

Wildfire cannot be classified as all good or all bad. Fire ecologists have proven that too much fire prevention is as harmful to our forests and wildlands as too little prevention. Ongoing studies are being made about the effects of wildfire on the environment.

A specially equipped helicopter starts a prescribed fire in California.

FIRE MANAGEMENT

As a result of the studies of fire ecologists, fire management techniques have been adjusted to allow healthy, controlled, periodic forest fires. In the United States, after decades of suppressing all wildfires, fire managers now acknowledge that some fire is beneficial to the environment. Firefighters no longer rush to extinguish a fire unless property or human life is threatened. Selected fires are allowed to burn themselves out.

Sometimes, prescribed fires (planned fires) are set to clear out dead vegetation or litter before it accidentally catches fire. Before setting a fire, firefighters study the weather. If conditions are right, a fire line is constructed around the entire area to be burned. Then a carefully controlled fire is set inside the fire line. This process eliminates the fuel that a wildfire needs to exist.

Prescribed fires help the environment in many ways. In addition to reducing the buildup of fuels, they improve the habitat for wildlife, help foresters control insects, return nutrients to the ground, and clean out logging slashes.

Controversy regarding how much we should interfere with natural forest fires raged after the 1988 Yellowstone fires. The 1988 controversy centered on the fire management policy that allows park officials to let natural fires burn, provided they are monitored daily and do not threaten property or human life.

Many critics believed that if the natural fires had been put out immediately, much of Yellowstone would have been spared. Others blamed the policy that the park officials had followed from the 1880s to the 1970s, which required that all fires be immediately extinguished. These critics maintained that this led to a dangerous buildup of dry, flammable vegetation on the forest floor. They claimed the park could have been saved by prescribed fires that would have reduced the amount of fuel in a controlled manner.

Bob Barbee, Yellowstone superintendent in 1988, believed that the media was unfair in its assessment of the Park

Service's natural fire policy. He stated that when drought conditions, an abundance of dead materials, high temperatures, and winds occur at the same time, such fires will flare up. They are a natural event beyond human control. Nevertheless, many media stories implied that the Park Service was at fault because of its "let burn" policy.

A firestorm rages out of control in Yellowstone National Park.

5

NEW CONCERNS

Your neighbors are on the move. Where are they going? To the country. Historically, wildfires have occurred in remote, sparsely populated areas. But as these previously unpopulated areas become more inhabited, this picture is changing. Since World War II, there has been a population shift from urban areas to suburban areas in the United States. During the 1970s, the rural population of the United States increased almost as fast as urban population. Improved transportation, an increase in two-income families, and more leisure time have prompted families to move away from the congestion of the city. This trend has increased the number of homes located in wildlands and created a new problem for wildland firefighters.

To many, the American Dream now includes a home in the country, surrounded by abundant shrubs and trees. As a result, large areas of the country contain expensive properties surrounded by flammable vegetation. This vegetation can be fodder for a wildland fire, turning the dream home into a nightmare.

A small fire crackles near a house in the woods. Houses surrounded by abundant vegetation can be vulnerable to wildfires.

THE WILDLAND-URBAN INTERFACE

The point at which wildland systems and urban systems meet and interact is called the interface. The wildland-urban interface is the area in which combustible homes meet combustible vegetation. The interface expands as the number of people living in the wilderness grows. Fires are a natural phenomenon in the wildlands, but people moving to these areas generally are not aware of the dangers from wildfire. They continue to build houses in forests, in scenic valleys, and in mountainous terrain with little regard for fire safety.

This situation poses many problems for fire managers. During a raging fire in Leavenworth, Washington, a seasoned firefighter observed: "When I started out, it seemed like all the fires were small, and we didn't have these urban interface problems. They just put us out with some C-rations [packages of prepared food used in emergencies] and we stayed until you couldn't stand each other or you put it out. We have much more knowledge, but the difficulty now is you just never seem to have a fire without the urban interface." Fire managers are now faced with the problem of protecting not only the forests, but the people and homes in nearby areas.

Certain well-populated parts of the country are especially prone to wildland fires. California is one of these areas. The climate in California creates one of the most fire-susceptible wildlands in the United States. California is warm and dry much of the year. The chaparral vegetation provides abundant fuel, and fires are often aided by hot, dry winds, called Santa Ana winds, that blow down the Sierra Nevada mountains from the northeast. These winds often reach sustained speeds of 60 to 80 miles per hour (97 to 129 km/hr), fanning any wildfires in progress. These conditions, combined with the large number of people moving into the wildlands, create a dangerous situation.

This danger led to a disaster in early October 1995 when a wildland fire swept along Inverness Ridge in Marin County, California. The fire burned 12,354 acres (5,000 hectares) of forest and brushland, and despite the efforts of over two thousand firefighters, the wildfire destroyed 45 homes in a

A house and truck devastated by the Inverness Ridge fire

community called Paradise Ranch Estates. In much of the community, only charred chimneys and smoldering car chassis remained. The fire was started by an illegal campfire built by four boys camping in the area. Though they attempted to extinguish the campfire by smothering it with dirt and rocks, the fire smoldered underground for two days before igniting the blaze. Nevertheless, citing the buildup of dry foliage in the area over a period of about sixty years, many inhabitants of the Inverness Ridge area believed that a devastating wildfire was just a matter of time. They blame the original real estate developers for irresponsibly building in a dangerous area.

Unfortunately, the Inverness Ridge fire was not an unusual or isolated event. In 1990, a wildfire near Santa Barbara consumed 4,900 acres (1,983 hectares), 427 homes, 221 apartments, and 10 public buildings. Between 1990 and 1993, approximately 4,500 structures were burned by wildfire in California.

Few populated areas of the United States must endure wildfires as frequently as California, but they can strike almost anywhere. During a severe dry spell at the end of August 1995, Suffolk County on Long Island, New York, was the site of a blaze for about three days. Though this area is not accustomed to wildfires, over two thousand firefighters were able to bring the fire under control with very little loss of property and no loss of life. The damage was especially light considering how densely the area is populated. Ultimately, the fire consumed about 6,000 acres (2,428 hectares) of pine forest and scrubland, 12 homes, and a few businesses. Strategic fire lines saved the most populated areas from destruction.

As more people move to the wildlands, more homes will be surrounded by vegetation that is potential fuel for a wild-

Firefighters protect this Suffolk County home from the nearby blaze.

fire. Unless people moving to the countryside respect the new fire dangers around them, the frequency and severity of fires will increase.

There are many precautions potential homeowners can take to protect themselves. They should choose a fire-safe location, checking to see what fire protection facilities are available. In less-congested areas, there are not fire hydrants on every corner. Owners should design and build a fire-safe structure. For example, untreated wood shingles should not be used. Chimneys and vents should be screened with incombustible wire mesh. After moving into the house, homeowners must continually maintain a fire-safe environment by stacking firewood away from the house, reducing the amount of vegetation surrounding the house, and keeping ample safety exits clear and accessible.

GLOBAL FIRE MANAGEMENT

Countries are now aware that sharing fire management information and resources is essential. Environmental problems, such as deforestation and the greenhouse effect, are of primary importance to all people of the world. Global cooperation on these matters is increasing.

The United States and Canada now have an agreement to share fire-fighting resources. In 1988, Canada sent 12 air tankers, 125 helicopter personnel, and nearly 4,200 Pulaskis to assist in fighting the wildfires that swept through the forests of the United States.

In 1989, at a global wildland fire conference in Boston, Massachusetts, three hundred fire experts from around the world attended conferences to help solve fire management problems. The United States government now conducts courses in fire management training in Chile and Mexico. On an international level, the United Nations Disaster Relief Organization seeks to reduce the effects of disasters such as wildfires.

With more people on the planet and less wildland preserved, wildfires in populated areas are increasing in frequency and severity. This is a global problem that must be addressed through fire research and cooperative fire management on an international level. We must all work together if we are to preserve our natural resources and protect the peoples of this earth.

FOR FURTHER READING

Lampton, Christopher. *Forest Fire*. Brookfield, CT: Millbrook Press, 1991.

Lauber, Patricia. *Summer of Fire: Yellowstone 1988*. New York: Orchard Books, 1991.

Poynter, Margaret. *Wildland Fire Fighting*. New York: Atheneum, 1982.

Pringle, Laurence P. *Natural Fire: Its Ecology in Forests*. New York: Morrow, 1979.

Vogt, Gregory. *Forests on Fire: The Fight to Save Our Trees*. New York: Franklin Watts, 1990.

Stewart, Gail. *Smokejumpers & Forest Firefighters*. Mankato, MN: Crestwood House, 1988.

INTERNET RESOURCES

Due to the changeable nature of the Internet, sites appear and disappear very quickly. The resources listed below offered useful information on wildfires at the time of publication. Internet addresses must be entered with capital and lower-case letters exactly as they appear.

The *Yahoo* directory of the World Wide Web is an excellent place to find Internet sites on any topic. The directory is located at: **http://www.yahoo.com**

The Federal Emergency Management Agency (FEMA) publishes wildfire safety guidelines on its Web site. It is located at: **http://www.fema.gov/fema/fact12.html**

The USDA Forest Service maintains a Web site at:
  http://www.fs.fed.us/Homepage.html

The following site offers a collection of photos showing a Hotshot team at work:
  http://www.sover.net/~kenandeb/fire/hotshot.html

INDEX

ABOUT THE AUTHOR

Ann Armbruster has been an English teacher and a school librarian. She is the author of Watts First Books *The American Flag*, *The United Nations, Tornadoes,* and *Floods*. Ms. Armbruster lives in Cambridge, Ohio.